HISTORIC
COMMUNITIES

spanish missions

Bobbie Kalman & Greg Nickles

Crabtree Publishing Company

www.crabtreebooks.com

HISTORIC
COMMUNITIES

Created by Bobbie Kalman

For my parents,
Joan and Ron Nickles

Editor-in-Chief
Bobbie Kalman

Writing team
Bobbie Kalman
Greg Nickles

Managing editor
Lynda Hale

Editors
Niki Walker
Petrina Gentile

Computer design
Lynda Hale

Consultant
Dr. Joseph P. Sanchez, Director, Spanish
Colonial Research Center, National Park
Service, Albuquerque, New Mexico

Special thanks to
Dr. James J. Miller and the Florida Division of Historical
Resources; Rosalind Rock and the San Antonio Missions
National Historical Park; National Park Service; Ann
Rasor and Pecos National Historical Park; the staff and
volunteers of Mission La Purísima Concepción
(California); Jim Graves, John Mione, Jacquie Nuñez,
and Mission San Juan Capistrano (California); Museum
of New Mexico; San Diego Historical Society

Separations and film
Dot 'n Line Image Inc.

Printer
Worzalla Publishing Company

Cover: The rebuilt church at the Taos Pueblo,
New Mexico

Title page: The church of Mission San Xavier
del Bac, Arizona

Crabtree Publishing Company
www.crabtreebooks.com   1-800-387-7650

Cataloging in Publication Data
Kalman, Bobbie, 1947-
  Spanish Missions

(Historic communities series)
Includes index.
ISBN 0-86505-436-3 (library bound) ISBN 0-86505-466-5 (pbk.)
This book examines daily life at missions during the Spanish colonial period in the
southern and southwestern United States.

1. Mission, Spanish - United States - Juvenile literature. 2. Catholic Church - Missions
- United States - Juvenile Literature. I. Nickels, Greg, 1969- . II. Title. III. Kalman,
Bobbie, 1947- . Historic Communities.

F799.K35 1996   j978   LC 96-26738
                                                                 CIP

**Published in
the United States**
PMB 16A
350 Fifth Ave.
Suite 3308
New York, NY
10118

**Published
in Canada**
616 Welland Ave.,
St. Catharines,
Ontario, Canada
L2M 5V6

**Published in the
United Kingdom**
73 Lime Walk
Headington
Oxford
0X3 7AD
United Kingdom

**Published
in Australia**
386 Mt. Alexander Rd.,
Ascot Vale (Melbourne)
V1C 3032

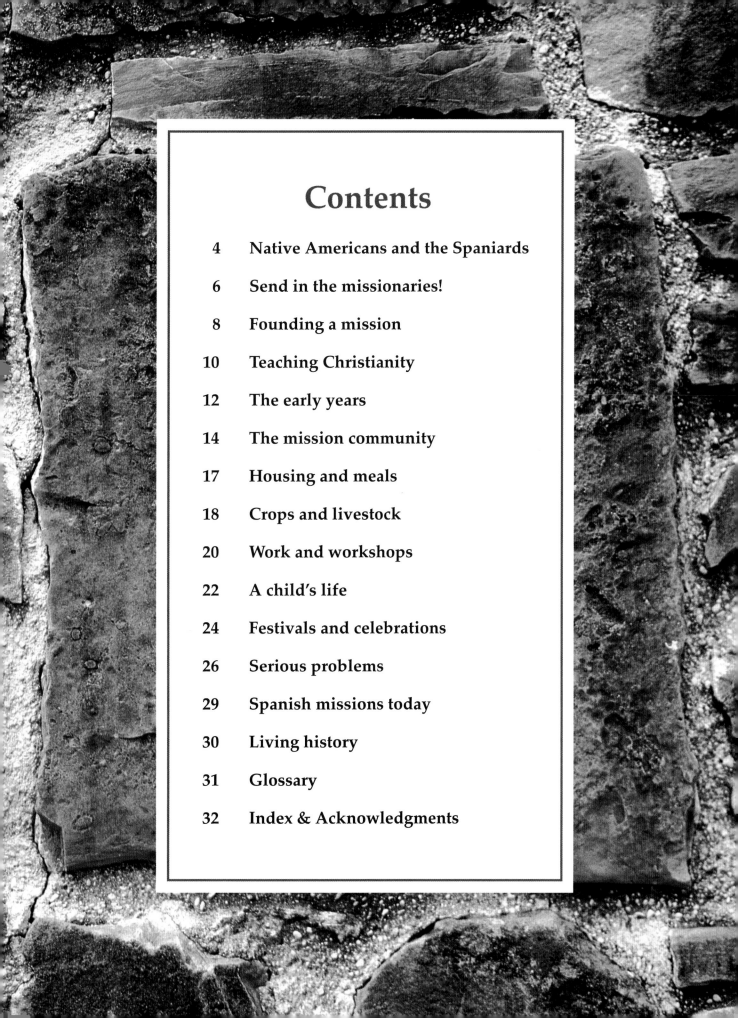

Contents

Native Americans and the Spaniards

Spain's king commanded powerful armies. He wanted to add new lands to his kingdom, so he provided explorers with ships in which to sail to unexplored areas. The pope, who is the leader of the Roman Catholic Church, sent priests to travel with the king's men.

In the 1400s, North and South America were very different than they are today. Countries such as the United States, Mexico, and Canada did not exist yet. Native Americans were the only people living in these areas. They lived in villages, towns, and cities and belonged to hundreds of different groups called **tribes**. Some tribes had thousands of members; others had only a few. Tribes had their own languages and customs.

Columbus sails to North America

Over 500 years ago, Europeans started sailing across the Atlantic Ocean in search of China and India. They wanted to bring back gold, silk, tea, dyes, spices, and other treasures. The king and queen of Spain gave ships and money to an Italian adventurer named Christopher Columbus so he could make such a voyage.

In 1492, Columbus set sail. When he arrived in North America, he was greeted by Native Americans. He called them Indians, mistakenly thinking he was near India. Although these peoples are still called Indians, most prefer to be known as Native Americans or to be called by the name of their tribe.

Conquering the New World

When Columbus returned and told the king and queen about the riches and peoples across the ocean, they sent more explorers and soldiers there. Before long, the kingdom of Spain claimed much of the land in North and South America.

Between the 1500s and the 1800s, Spanish priests started hundreds of **missions** *in what is now the United States. At the missions, the priests taught Native Americans about Christianity. This map shows some of the places where Spanish missions were once located.*

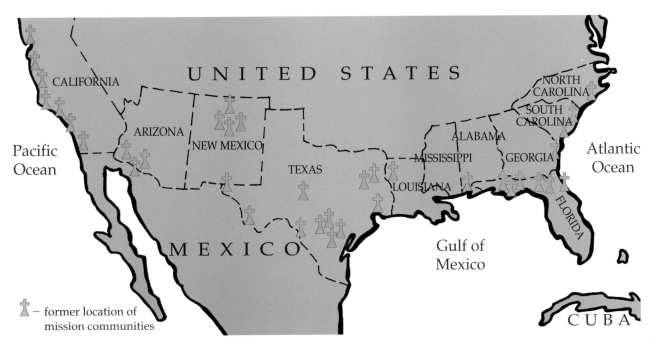

- former location of mission communities

Send in the missionaries!

Spain was a Christian kingdom. Its powerful priests convinced the king to send **missionaries** to the New World to teach Native Americans about Jesus Christ, whom Christians believe is the Son of God. The king also hoped that missionaries would convince the people of the tribes to become Spanish subjects.

A missionary used holy water to baptize people who wanted to become Christian.

Who were missionaries?

Missionaries were men who gave up their personal belongings and devoted their lives to teaching about Christianity. Spanish missionaries belonged to a powerful Christian church called the Roman Catholic Church. They were known as priests or **padres**, which means "father" in Spanish. Many padres were well educated and spent years studying the Bible. They also learned about agriculture, construction, and various trades to help them survive in faraway lands.

The duties of a missionary

In addition to teaching and studying, missionaries performed Christian ceremonies. Two of the most important ceremonies were **baptism** and **communion**. Baptism is a ceremony that involves pouring holy water on a person as a sign of admission into the Christian faith. Communion, a sharing of holy bread and wine, celebrates the sacrifice of Jesus Christ's life for his followers.

The padres wore long robes of rough fabric tied at the waist with a cord or rope.

(top) Missionaries used bells to signal when it was time to eat, work, rest, or worship.

Founding a mission

All that was needed to **found**, or start, a mission was a missionary to teach Christian beliefs and a community of Native Americans willing to learn them. The Spanish priests also wanted to teach the tribes to live European-style. Changing people's beliefs and their way of life required years of work, so the padres needed shelter and a supply of food. The **site**, or location, of a new mission was carefully chosen with the help of maps and explorers' reports. It had to be near a Native American settlement, fertile farmland, a plentiful water supply, and building materials such as stones, trees, and clay.

To reach a mission site, some padres had to walk hundreds of miles without guides or the protection of soldiers.

8

The padres prepare

After the site was chosen, one or two padres were selected to run the new mission. Some founded their mission by themselves. Many, however, enlisted the aid of Spanish soldiers, artisans, and settlers. They collected necessary supplies such as seeds, tools, and clothing and packed books, bells, and sacred vessels for the future church. They took along cattle, horses, sheep, and other livestock as sources of food, wool, and labor. The padres also brought with them food and gifts to share with the Native Americans.

Some missionaries traveled with large groups of Spanish settlers and soldiers.

Difficult journeys

The padres, their helpers, and supplies were taken across the water by ship or overland to the mission site by pack train. The journey was often so dangerous that livestock, supplies, and people were lost along the way. Deadly storms and illnesses such as scurvy plagued the sea voyagers. On land, the travelers suffered from exhaustion and faced attacks by unfriendly tribes.

The founding ceremony

After arriving at the site, the padres dedicated the new mission by building an altar and performing a special ceremony. Sometimes a timber cross was erected on the location of the future church. The padres then blessed the site with a sprinkling of holy water.

The padres hoped their ceremonies and offers of food and gifts would attract the Native Americans. They could not speak the local language at first and had to communicate with the nearby tribe using hand signs.

In a mission church, a neophyte receives a blessing from a priest.

Confession *was a Roman Catholic practice introduced to the Native Americans. A priest sat inside a booth and listened to a convert admit his "sins."*

Teaching Christianity

The padres felt their most important job was to teach about Christianity. Although many Native Americans accepted Christianity, they did not want to abandon their traditional beliefs.

Native American beliefs

In the thousands of years before the padres arrived, Native Americans practiced their own beliefs. The different tribes did not follow one religion, as the padres did. Instead, each tribe believed in its own gods and spirits who were thought to live inside humans, animals, trees, plants, the earth, the sky, and water.

Most Native Americans believed that acts such as growing food or killing animals could annoy the spirits and upset the balance of nature. When nature was unbalanced, problems such as droughts, floods, and disease occurred. Ceremonies that included dancing, music, and singing were held to make peace with the spirits.

What is a neophyte?

Native Americans who accepted Christian teachings and came to live at the mission were called **converts** or **neophytes**. The padres expected neophytes to learn Spanish, dress European-style, help with the work, and pray and worship with them.

Why did Native Americans convert?

Although life with the missionaries was not easy, thousands of Native Americans eventually became converts. Some neophytes believed in the Christian religion. Others felt they had no choice but to convert—they came to the mission seeking food or protection from hostile settlers, soldiers, and enemy tribes.

Every Native American dealt differently with the padres. Many welcomed them, but others worried that the missionaries would change the old ways. Each padre was different as well. Some were strict or cruel, but others were kind.

The early years

Mission San Luis in Florida, shown above, had many buildings including a large, round Native American council house.

This hut at Mission San Juan Capistrano in California was made from reeds and branches.

Each mission had its own name and history. Some made many converts and prospered for decades; others lasted only a few months. Almost all, however, began with a few rough shelters built quickly from whatever materials could be found. Walls were constructed from reeds, branches, or poles and plastered with clay. Roofs were **thatched** with grass and mud. With help from Native Americans, the padres cleared farmland, built fences, and dug ditches to direct water to the mission from a nearby river or stream.

Dangerous beginnings

The first years at a mission were often difficult. Many missionaries and their helpers had to live without proper food or tools. When supplies failed to arrive, some people starved to death. The weather caused hardships as well. Droughts and floods killed crops and livestock, leaving the mission with little food. During these hard times, some Native Americans left the missionaries. Others stayed and helped the padres survive.

Forced to stay

After working with the priests, many Native Americans became converts and came to live at the mission. Before long, however, some of these converts grew tired of the strict rules and daily routine. They wanted to leave, but the priests feared that the converts would forget Christianity once they were away from the mission. Sometimes guards, who were either neophytes or soldiers, were posted to stop the converts from leaving. Those who tried to escape were punished with a whipping.

The wood and thatch church at Mission San Luis had a rectangular shape like the churches in Europe.

The mission community

*The quadrangle at Mission Concepción in Texas was formed by the church, houses, workshops, and open area. The church's towers could be seen from far down the **Camino Real**, the Spanish road that connected the mission to other settlements.*

This photograph shows ruins of an old mission quadrangle.

As a mission grew, new buildings were constructed. Materials such as wood, thatch, clay, stone, brick, tiles, and a cement made of burned seashells and sand were used to build the new structures.

Plazas and quadrangles

The mission's main buildings were constructed around a large open area in which people played and gathered for special events. In the eastern regions, these open areas, called **plazas**, were often round. In the western regions, the open area, workshops, houses, and mission church were sometimes arranged in a square called a **quadrangle**. The buildings of a quadrangle formed four walls, so the mission could be defended easily if someone attacked from the outside. The doors and windows faced the open area, allowing the padres and guards to watch the neophytes as they worked.

The mission church

The mission church was the tallest of all the buildings and was crowned with crosses of wood or iron. Some churches had statues near their decorated entrance doors. Many buildings were also painted in bright colors and patterns. Inside, murals covered the ceilings and walls with scenes from the Bible. Priests performed ceremonies at an altar, which was located at one end of the building.

Services at the mission

Besides a church, workrooms, and houses, many other buildings were constructed. Hospital rooms, or **infirmaries**, were set up to house the sick and injured. Animal hides were cured at the **tannery**, and cloth was woven at the **weaving house**. Storerooms housed tools, equipment, and supplies, and **granaries** stored seeds and grain.

The outside of Mission Concepción's church was painted with bright designs. The mission's well and cemetery were located in front of the church. At some missions, the cemetery was under the church floor.

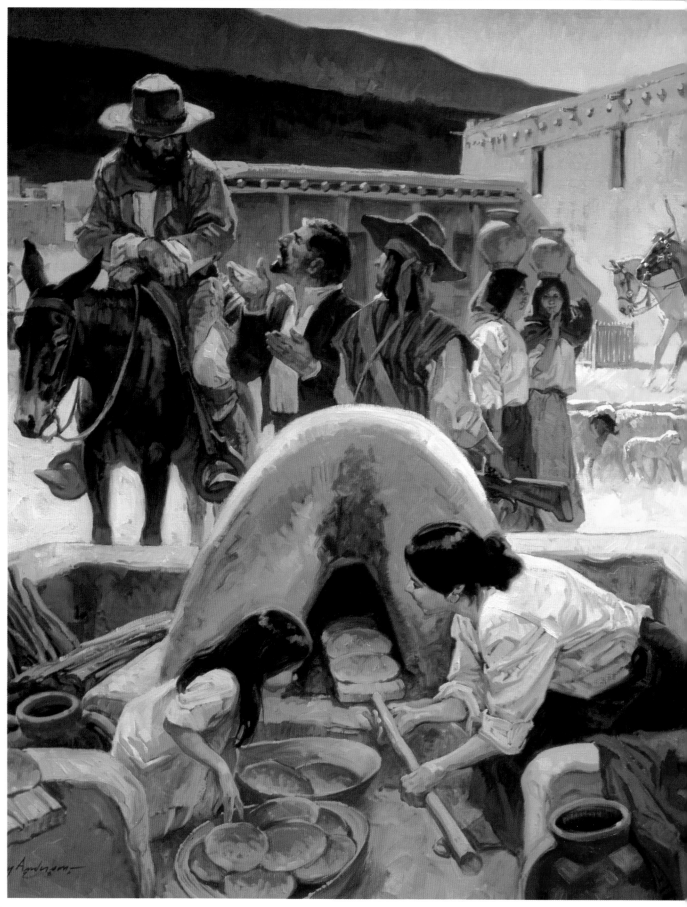

Housing and meals

Priests, guards, and neophytes had a variety of houses, or **living quarters**. The quarters were mainly used for sleeping, eating, and doing household chores. The rooms were dark and had only a few furnishings. Mattresses were stuffed with straw and often became infested with fleas.

Living and guest quarters

Priests and guards were housed in buildings close to the church. Guests visited frequently and stayed in rooms next to those of the priests. Married neophytes, their children, and the elderly lived in a village away from the padres. Sometimes boys, girls, and unmarried women had to live apart from the village in special quarters where they were watched by the padres' helpers.

Mission meals

Native American girls and women prepared foods over an open fire or in ovens made of stone, brick, or clay. Most meals were made with corn flour, milk and, sometimes, beef. Many missions offered only a small selection of foods, so converts had to search for other nutrition in the wild. Prosperous missions, however, served many types of foods.

At this mission, artisans are busy making crafts, boys are tending the animals, girls and women are baking bread, and visiting traders are bartering for grain, livestock, hides, and crafts.

Crops and livestock

Growing crops was one of the more important tasks at a mission. The padres wanted to raise enough food to feed everyone. Neophytes worked hard to ensure that a daily supply of grain, fruit, and vegetables was available.

Planting season

In the spring, neophytes prepared the soil with hand tools or plows drawn by teams of oxen. They then dropped beans, lentils, and peas in rows and planted corn in small hills called **furrows**. Gardens and orchards were grown close to the mission buildings and were fenced to keep out hungry humans and animals.

All by hand

Neophytes tended the growing crops closely, making sure they were watered and weeded. Harvests were especially busy times. All the grains, fruits, and vegetables were picked by hand and hauled to the storage buildings in baskets and ox-drawn carts.

Irrigation ditches such as this one moved water from rivers and streams to the missions. The water was used for washing, watering crops and, at some missions, for powering a gristmill.

Horses did not pull carts or plows. Instead, oxen performed these important tasks.

Raising livestock

Animals were very important. Horses were used to transport people and goods. The hides of cattle were made into leather, and their fat was boiled down for candles and soap. The wool of sheep was used to make clothes. Although cattle, sheep, and horses were the main livestock, neophytes often tended a variety of other animals, including pigs, poultry, and goats. All these animals were a source of meat.

Slaughtering season

The neophytes spent long hours feeding, guarding, herding, and branding the mission livestock. Summer was the slaughtering season. It was the mission's busiest time—hundreds of animals were butchered for their meat, fat, and hides.

Even though padres taught European methods of farming, many missions relied on the Native American skills of hunting and gathering food.

Some missions became famous for the horses they raised.

Work and workshops

Besides farming, Native Americans performed many other jobs at the missions. Spanish artisans taught the men carpentry, blacksmithing, leather working, and construction. Women learned European-style pottery making, weaving, spinning, candle making, and cooking.

The tannery and leather shops

Before hides could be used to make leather products, they were hauled to the tannery. There, they were cleaned, soaked, and rubbed with oils to make them soft. The leather was then taken to workshops where it was fashioned into sacks, pouches, clothing, reins, and saddles.

Hides were stretched either on a frame or on the ground, where they were held with pegs.

(top) Workers hauled stones from the quarry to build a mission church.

The weaving house

At the weaving house, wool was carded, spun, and woven into fabric for clothes, mats, and bedding. Most Native Americans knew how to weave before the Spaniards arrived. The padres, however, introduced new methods of spinning and weaving, using European spinning wheels and looms.

Brick and tile making

Some neophytes had the job of making bricks and tiles. To make bricks, soil or clay was blended with bits of straw or grass in a trough. Water was added, and the mud was mixed until it became stiff. The mud was then shaped in a mold and left in the sun to dry. After several days, the bricks hardened and were ready to use in construction. Roof and floor tiles were made from clay in a similar way.

Candles and soap

One of the ingredients in candles and soap was **tallow**, a hard fat from slaughtered animals. To make candles, long strings were hung over a stick and dipped many times in a vat of melted tallow. As each layer of fat hardened around the string, the candles grew thicker. Soap was made by boiling tallow and lye together in a big iron pot. When cool, the hardened soap was cut into bars.

Pottery making

Clay pots and jars were used every day to carry water and to store food such as grain. Pottery making was an ancient skill practiced by both Native Americans and Spaniards. At the missions, women crafted pots and jars as well as bowls, candlesticks, and other useful objects.

In addition to agriculture and craft making, daily work included collecting firewood, fetching water, looking after young children, and washing clothes.

A child's life

Life was difficult and confusing for children at the missions. They were raised both by their parents, who taught them Native American customs, and the padres, who taught them European ways. In addition to their duties as students, children were expected to help with many chores.

Divided families

Some priests wanted to prevent parents from teaching Native American traditions to their children. They forced the children to live in separate quarters away from their parents. Boys were housed in one building and girls in another. To ensure they behaved, an older person watched the children while they ate and slept.

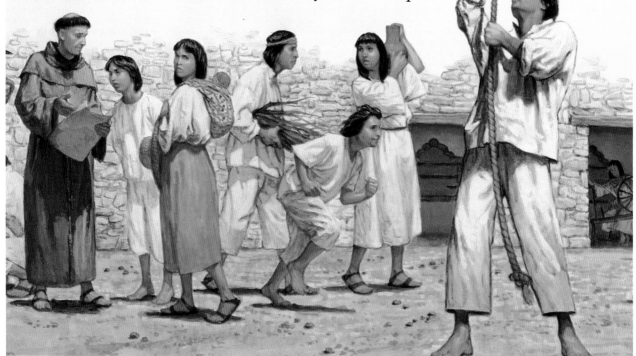

Education and training

Every day at the sound of a bell, children assembled to learn the Spanish language and Christian teachings from the padres. Girls were given instruction in European manners. They were also taught to cook, sew, and make pottery. Many learned how to spin and weave.

Some of the boys became apprentices to artisans such as tanners, blacksmiths, carpenters, and painters. A few received singing, flute, violin, or guitar lessons. The boys who were selected to learn hymns and play instruments were also taught to read and write.

Doing chores

In addition to lessons and other work, boys and girls were assigned chores. Some of the boys acted as servants to the padres and had special duties at the church. A few were chosen to ring the mission bells or guard drying bricks from the feet of stray animals. Both girls and boys helped with the livestock and with harvesting fruits, vegetables, and other crops.

Time for play

In their free time, children enjoyed playing with friends and family. A guest at one mission in California wrote that the game of *takersia* was popular. Players used long sticks to try and catch a small hoop that was rolled along the ground. A guessing game called *toussi* was also fun to play. Players tried to hide a piece of wood in one hand while making all sorts of confusing gestures. Other players tried to guess in which hand the wood was hidden. Whenever possible, adults played these games with their children.

When their work was finished, children played together or amused themselves. They had few toys, so they made up games using sticks, stones, and other common objects.

Festivals and celebrations

Celebrations were a welcome break from the daily work routines of priests and neophytes. Christmas and Easter were the biggest Christian festivals, but smaller celebrations were held on other holy days throughout the year.

Most priests tried to stop the converts from performing traditional Native American ceremonies, so these were usually held in secret. Eventually, some padres allowed the celebrations. Wearing masks and special clothing, celebrants danced, sang, and played games.

Music and drama

Neophyte choirs and musicians performed at church services regularly and practiced special hymns and chants for festivals. For Christmas, performers prepared religious plays such as the *Pastorela*, in which they re-enacted Mary and Joseph's journey to Bethlehem. At the end of this play, the Nativity scene was presented, and the audience was invited to view a figure of the Christ Child.

Ring the bells!

Many missions had *esquilas*, which were bells that turned completely over. On special occasions, a boy climbed to the top of the bell tower and rang these joyous, musical bells. Using his hands, he pushed the bottom of a bell away from him until he could reach its top. Then, grasping the top, he gave it a great downward shove and sent the bell spinning. Ringing the *esquilas* required practice. If the boy was not careful, the bell could swing around and knock him off his feet!

Some bells were rung by tugging a rope tied to the bell's clapper.

The spinning bells in this mission church are called **esquilas**.

Padres tried to stop neophytes from holding Native American ceremonies. A few priests, however, allowed traditional masks and costumes to be worn during Christian festival plays.

Serious problems

Native Americans and Spaniards often cooperated peacefully in work and worship at the missions. Still, troubles such as arguments, violence, and illness arose. In many cases, these problems led to the abandonment or destruction of a mission settlement.

Struggling with traditions

The padres thought they could improve the lives of Native Americans by teaching them about Christianity. They tried to change Native American traditions by forcing the people to worship Jesus Christ, speak Spanish, and dress in European-style clothing. Those who did not cooperate were whipped or put in stocks and chains. For years, Native Americans struggled to avoid these painful punishments and preserve their valuable traditions.

Padres, soldiers, and the many Native Americans who died of illnesses were buried in the mission cemetery.

Deadly diseases

When the Europeans came to North America, they unknowingly brought diseases that killed millions of Native Americans. Sometimes entire tribes were wiped out by epidemics. Death due to sickness was part of daily life at most missions. Malnutrition, caused by a lack of nutritious foods, was also a problem that frequently led to death. Many infirmaries were filled with sick and dying people. At some missions, so many converts died that the settlements eventually became deserted.

Under attack

Violence and war destroyed many missions and killed thousands of people. Some tribes, such as the Pueblos of New Mexico, became hostile toward the Spaniards and drove them away. British soldiers also attacked and destroyed many Spanish settlements in North America.

Many padres insisted that Spanish soldiers live outside the missions in nearby forts called **presidios.** *The priests did not trust the soldiers, but they relied on them to capture escaped neophytes and stop Native American protests.*

San Francisco de Asis in New Mexico has been the subject of many famous paintings and photographs.

Christian services are still held in the long, narrow church at Mission San Juan in Texas.

The Alamo, a famous fort from the 1830s, was originally a mission called San Antonio de Valero.

Spanish missions today

In 1821, Mexico became a country and took over the Spanish missions in North America. Eventually, most mission lands were divided up by Mexican and American settlers. Some padres and converts tried to stay at the missions, but their houses and churches fell into disrepair. Many mission sites were finally abandoned.

Today, a number of mission churches and buildings have been restored. They are used by the Roman Catholic Church, the National Park Service, and descendants of the Spaniards and Native Americans who once lived at the missions. Historians and tourists visit the old sites to explore and imagine what daily life was like during the years of Spanish rule.

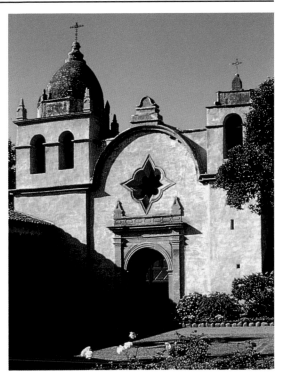

The Carmel Mission, now restored, was once the central mission in California.

Visitors believe that the small church at El Sanctuario de Chimayo, New Mexico, is a place of healing.

Living history

Old missions throughout the United States hold living-history days, during which people dress in costume and re-enact the lives of missionaries, soldiers, artisans, and Native Americans. Perhaps you have visited an old mission and watched historic guides spin yarn, make candles, or weave rugs. Historic re-enactments offer us a fascinating look at the work, good times, and struggles that took place at the Spanish missions many years ago.

(top) Visitors can watch re-enactments at Mission La Purísima Concepción in California.
(bottom) A young New Mexican girl shows how to bake bread the traditional way.

Glossary

altar In a Christian church, the table where sacred vessels are placed and bread and wine blessed

apprentice A person who learns a skill by working with an artisan

artisan A skilled tradesperson

baptism A Christian ceremony in which a person is blessed with holy water to show his or her admission into the Christian faith

ceremony An act or set of acts performed on an important occasion

Christianity A religion based on the teachings of Jesus Christ

communion A Christian ceremony in which bread and wine are consumed to celebrate the sacrifice of Jesus' life

community A group of people who live in one area and share buildings, services, and a way of life; also the place where these people live

convert (noun) A person who has changed his or her beliefs; (verb) to cause someone to change beliefs

explorer A person who travels to discover other lands, seas, or peoples

granary A building where grain is stored

gristmill A mill that grinds grain

hide An animal's skin

holy water Water blessed by a priest

infirmary A room or building used for the care of injured and sick people

irrigation A system by which dry land is supplied with water

lye A solution made by pouring water over wood ashes

Native Americans People whose ancestors were the first to live on the continents of North and South America

Nativity scene Figures including Mary, Joseph, and the baby Jesus, set in a stable

neophyte A person who has converted to a religion

New World A term used by Europeans to refer to North and South America

pack train Mules, horses, or other strong animals that are loaded with supplies and travel in a long line

priest A person in the Roman Catholic Church who devotes his life to religion and performs religious ceremonies

quadrangle An open area and the buildings around it that form a square

quarters Housing

Roman Catholicism A system of Christian churches, priests, and followers headed by the pope

sacred vessel A special container used in religious ceremonies

scurvy A disease caused by a lack of vitamin C

settler A person who makes his or her home in a new land or territory

sin An act that breaks the rules of a religion

Spain A country in southwest Europe

stocks A wooden frame that has holes for holding a person's ankles

subject A person who is under the control of a king or queen

tannery A place where hides are made into soft leather

thatch Long grasses, reeds, or straw used to cover a roof

tradition A custom that is handed down from one generation to another

tribe A group of people with common ancestry, language, and culture

Index

Acknowledgments

Photographs and reproductions
Ben Barnhart: page 26
John Boykin: page 24
John Cancalosi/Tom Stack & Associates: title page, page 30 (bottom)
Gerald Corsi/Tom Stack & Associates: cover, page 29 (bottom)
Jim Graves: pages 7, 12
Grady H. Harrison Jr.: pages 3, 14, 28 (bottom left & right)
Brian Parker/Tom Stack & Associates: page 28 (top)
Tom Stack/Tom Stack & Associates: page 29 (top)
Tony Zinnanti: pages 10 (both), 18 (both), 19, 20, 30 (top)

Illustrations
Gil Cohen, courtesy of the National Park Service: pages 4, 6, 7, 8, 9 (bottom), 14, 15, 19, 20, 21, 24, 25, 27
Florida Division of Historical Resources: pages 12, 13
Pecos National Historical Park, copyright Roy Andersen: pages 9 (top), 11, 16-17
Richard Williams, courtesy of the National Park Service: pages 22, 23

5 6 7 8 9 0 Printed in the U.S.A. 5